MY BO
MY BODY
EARS

AMY CULLIFORD

T0011482

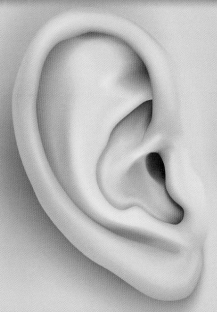

A Crabtree Roots Plus Book

CRABTREE
Publishing Company
www.crabtreebooks.com

School-to-Home Support for Caregivers and Teachers

This book helps children grow by letting them practice reading. Here are a few guiding questions to help the reader with building his or her comprehension skills. Possible answers appear here in red.

Before Reading:

- What do I think this book is about?
  - *I think this book is about my ears.*
  - *I think this book is about how we use our ears to hear.*
- What do I want to learn about this topic?
  - *I want to learn about the parts of an ear.*
  - *I want to learn about how ears hear sounds.*

During Reading:

- I wonder why...
  - *I wonder why I have one ear on each side of my head.*
  - *I wonder why some people cannot hear.*
- What have I learned so far?
  - *I have learned that some people have large ears and others have small ears.*
  - *I have learned that ears can hear loud and quiet sounds.*

After Reading:

- What details did I learn about this topic?
  - *I have learned that my brain tells me what I am hearing.*
  - *I have learned that some people use hearing aids to help them hear.*
- Read the book again and look for the vocabulary words.
  - *I see the word **quiet** on page 12 and the word **deaf** on page 17. The other vocabulary words are found on page 23.*

You have two **ears**.

There is one ear on each side of your head!

Ears can be big or small.

Do you hear that?

I hear a song!

Your ears help you hear.

Your **brain** tells you what you are hearing!

Your ears help you
hear **quiet** sounds.

Your ears help you
hear **loud** sounds too!

Your ears help you find where a sound comes from.

I can hear the
cat meow!

Some people cannot hear sounds. They are **deaf**.

They might use **hearing aids** to help them hear better.

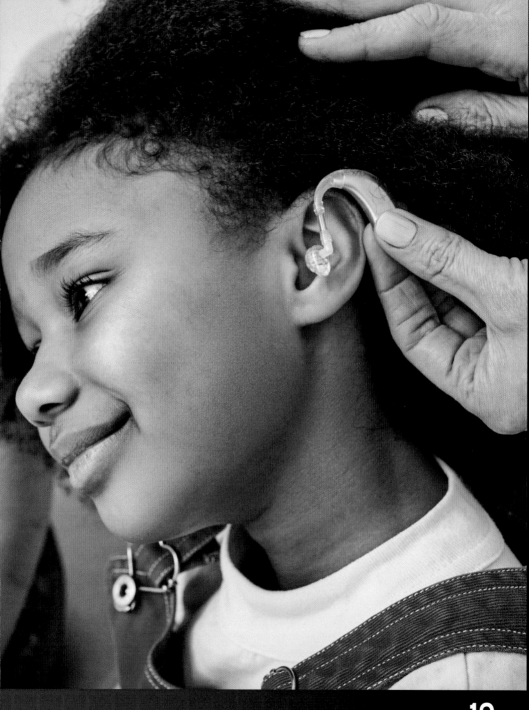

I use my ears
every day!

Word List
Sight Words

a	hearing	tells
are	help	that
be	I	the
big	is	there
can	might	they
cat	my	too
comes	of	two
day	on	use
do	one	what
each	or	where
every	people	you
find	side	your
from	small	
have	some	
head	song	
hear	sound	

Words to Know

brain

deaf

ears

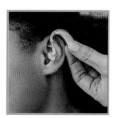

hearing aids

loud

quiet

MY BODY
MY BODY HAS
EARS

Written by: Amy Culliford

Designed by: Rhea Wallace

Series Development: James Earley

Proofreader: Janine Deschenes

Educational Consultant: Marie Lemke M.Ed.

Print and production coordinator:

Katherine Berti

Photographs:
Shutterstock: Matt Hahnewald: cover, p. 3; Larysa
Dubinska: p. 4; Prostock-studio: p. 5; Africa Studio: p. 7,
16; Wavebreakmedia: p. 8; Allsald: p. 9; Sutadimages: p.
11; Alexander Jitarev: p. 12; Galyna Andrushko: p. 15; Insta_
photos: p. 17; Peakstock: p. 19; ESB Professional: p. 21

Library and Archives Canada Cataloguing in Publication

Available at the Library and Archives Canada

Library of Congress Cataloging-in-Publication Data

Available at the Library of Congress

Crabtree Publishing Company

www.crabtreebooks.com   1-800-387-7650

Printed in the U.S.A./CG20210915/012022

Published in the United States
Crabtree Publishing
347 Fifth Avenue, Suite 1402-145
New York, NY, 10016

Published in Canada
Crabtree Publishing
616 Welland Ave.
St. Catharines, Ontario L2M 5V6